Water ~ Dreaming

Deirdre Grace Callanan

Water~Dreaming

Poems by

Deirdre Grace Callanan

Bass River Press

South Yarmouth, Massachusetts

Copyright © 2018 by Deirdre Callanan
All rights reserved

No part of this book may be reproduced, stored in a database or other retrieval system, or transmitted in any form, by any means, including mechanical, electronic, photocopy, recording or otherwise, without the prior written permission of the publisher.

Printed by Lightning Source, Inc.
Edited by Angela Howes
Interior Design and Composition by Angela Howes
Cover art by Heather Karp

Published by Bass River Press
307 Old Main St.
South Yarmouth, MA 02664
www.cultural-center.org

An imprint of the Cultural Center of Cape Cod, Bass River Press was launched in 2014 to support literary artists from the Cape & Islands – and has since devoted itself to publishing one book of poetry per year. Former Poet Laureate of Rhode Island Lisa Starr judged the 2017 poetry competition and selected Deirdre Callanan's manuscript for publication.

Library of Congress Control Number: 2017963803

CULTURAL CENTER
OF CAPE COD
All the Arts for All of Us

Contents:

Currents ~ 1602 1

I. August 1938 ~ December 1942 3
Then Wind 5
The Springfield Morning Union 6
ENFIELD 7
Wisps 8
As If 9
She Learns 10
Asa J. Snow 11
Cranberry Wreath 12

II. August 1937 ~ July 1938 15
Gramps let me choose 17
first day of our last year 18
Touching Quabbin Park Cemetery 19
Shawl 22
Suddenly, the Body 23
Gutted 24
Amber 25
vowed not to cut my hair 26
Dana's Last Concert 27
Farewell Ball 28
at 12:01 a.m. 29
Opening Day 30
Irises 31
Mrs. Munroe lowered the flag 32
I'm immersed 33
from BOBBIN HOLLOW 34
E.D. ~ C.S. 36
no parade 37

III. Spring 1943 ~ Summer 1946 39
Adelaide 41
Popcorn Snow 42
Sleight 45
Flora Howe 46

A Word That Breathes	48
Annie E. Doane	49
Isn't It Time	50
A Sudden Freight of Wind	52
Pale Scar	53
Dawn Prior	54
What Was Said	56
IV. 1947 ~ ~ ~	**59**
At Last	61
At First	62
Hollyhocks	63
All Afternoon	64
Water-boatman	65
((((Halo))))	66
Finding Swift River	67
A Door Opens	68
Vespers	69
Currents	70

Dear Reader:

Water~Dreaming draws from the history of the destruction of the Swift River Valley in western Massachusetts during the 1930s. Although Cora Snow is my invention, many of the events and characters in her world are based on records from that time.

In order to provide water for Boston, the 1927 Swift River Act authorized a reservoir's construction. Towns were emptied of their people, both the living and those buried. Buildings were removed or razed. Vegetation was cleared, its remains burned.

The mammoth engineering project ensued, and by the fall of 1938 the area was evacuated. Flooding began on August 14, 1939. It took seven years for Quabbin Reservoir to fill to its capacity of 412,000,000,000 gallons.

The Swift River Valley's rivers, streams, and brooks were often described as being of "almost prehistoric clarity and taste." Eight decades later, the lake continues to be an essential source of greater Boston's water supply.

The losses to the former families of Dana, Enfield, Greenwich, Prescott, and nearby villages remain immeasurable.

~For my parents~

*It is easy to descend into Avernus.
Death's dark door
stands open day and night.
But to retrace your steps
and get back to upper air,
That is the task,
that is the undertaking.*

"Aeneid Book VI," Virgil

translated by Seamus Heaney

Currents ~ 1602

NaniQuaben lays the perch
on Pottapaug's bank
wipes his spear

He nods to the hills
where the lake was born
bows to the river's branches

to the glistening valley
the Nipmuc call *Quaben* –
the meeting of many waters

Tilting his face to the sky
he gives thanks

The sachem guides his stag west
dissolves

I. August 1938 ~ December 1942

Then Wind

sniffs
the girl's breath
curious

        Wind like graphite
        wanton Wind, ravenous

                Wind of poplar's tenacity
                of rake tines on stone

Wind who contrives with oak
a flawless syllogism

        flattering Wind,
        arrogant, cunning

                Wind with nightshade's sheen
                impatient Wind, ruthless

Wind lonely as the inside of a bell

        Remorseless, unchaste Wind
        which ravages, indiscriminate

                Wind whose throat
                grown slick as wasps
                inhales

                translates her
                to red clover

which sparks
isolate
desolate

The Springfield Morning Union

August 25, 1938

ENFIELD – **Fire Claims Local Girl**

Cora Snow, 14, burned to death yesterday on the town green as the result of a fire-pit accident.

The valiant efforts of her brother, Will, 11, and of their friend Bun Doubleday, 15, failed to save Miss Snow. Dr. Willard B. Segur pronounced her dead at 6:30 p.m.

The few remaining valley residents rallied around the distraught young men and the grandfather, Josiah Snow.

The family collie, sorely injured during the rescue attempt, is expected to survive.

The bereft family had endured a prior devastating loss in 1934. Mr. Snow's son, Calvin, and his daughter-in-law, Cora, went missing while sailing in the Ionian Sea off the island of Kerkyra. After a lengthy search, Greek officials declared the couple lost at sea.

Miss Snow's memorial details will appear in this afternoon's Springfield Union.

ENFIELD

Cora Snow, 14, died on Enfield Green yesterday, as the result of a fire.

Daughter of the late Calvin W. and Cora (Doane) Snow, she was born at Enfield August 24, 1924. She is survived by her brother, William, and her grandfather, Josiah C. Snow.

The funeral will be held in St. Mary's Church, Ware, Sunday at 2 p.m. Burial will be in Quabbin Park Cemetery.

August 28, 1938

Wisps

*If an owl appeared in that birch,
a fox stepped through this rain,*

*but one does not appear,
does not step through.*

*Gathered at the rim,
they lay lilies on her grave.*

*Wisps of her other self
& one charred ring –*

*wrapped in a quilt square,
locked in a tin.*

1939

As If

    she   Wanders

          in   a   dark Wood

                of   scrambled

                      Chokecherry

Hemlocks

        &   Burrs

            with   neither

                    Path to   Lead

nor Hand

        to Guide

                        Not   Even

                        Hers

1940

She Learns

to twist
  among soiltunnels/
pleatedroots/
  mossswards/

to thrust
  past earthrind/
past figures
           stalled
  (gossamer friezes)
above
      cherubs
        &
    Death-heads/

to swivel
       helter-skelter
t/h/r/o/u/g/h   pines/

to navigate
       a charged terrain/
these rows
       her village   where
    LightStreams
        in
      columns
from certain graves
(their markers plinths)/

       that only some
       stonesGlow//

October 1941

+ Asa J. Snow

B 1797 ~ D 1872

  stare marker
        he sweeps through

attentive   none yet has
spectacles   suit   gaunt

queer vocal
       try

-Cora Snow. Related?
      Probably

-Father…Calvin
      born, raised Enfield

After my time
      he hard looks

It's difficult at first
     -guess learn

don't know expect
     Neither do I, even now

he   **whooooshes**
     fairy-tale

Bun! 3 tiny pumpkins
     headstone

Oh oh oh   if could but   reach

Christmas 1942

Cranberry Wreath

over frozen fields
        carols   *Bóg Się Rodzi*

nuns' first Mass
        St. Mary's… here come

my darlings   Shawl
        collar bell tinkle

Gramps   thin   clutches wreath
        as if tractor wheel

brother eyes my snowdrop
        dear Will – older now than I ever

 soft stirrings
        faint shifts

Shawl stretches on my stone
        muzzle on paws

Will starts to pull
        Gramps   *It's all right*

music fades
        naught to say

regret's force
        pinches like a vise

wreath   thick-berried
        garnet-fierce

II. August 1937 ~ July 1938

Gramps let me choose

my birthday present (August 24, 1937) =
Blossom, my perky Auracana, who'll lay celery-hued eggs*

Will surprised me with moleskin journals, soft as
Violet's muzzle — I'll devote the mauve one to poems.
This one's for the flood of changes in our lives…

4 Augusts ago, Mama & Pa gave me the Aeneid —
those winter evenings by the stove
passing the book back & forth between us…

This map of Greece tacked to my closet door
might as well be Mars

first day of our last year

in this school, September 6,
Miss Rugg gave an assignment due next June!?!

I'm to make a list of memories that tug at my heart —
how might I represent them?

Will had the same homework — our teachers in cahoots
just like that he decided to build a model
but I swing back & forth like Uncle Parker's clock

*mural / quilt \ collage / quilt *

(when they sunk shaft 12 for the new reservoir,
Uncle Parker let his clock run down,
fixed it to the wall as a brace against blasts.
Silly but fun when Pa + Uncle Parker used to harmonize
with that grandfather's clock song on the radio)

once we move to Amherst I might build a clock
a magic one ~ ~ ~ so I can go back to when…

Touching Quabbin Park Cemetery

With folks in a swivet over the demolition commotion,
we high-tail it to the QPC when we can,

pass between Mr. Frier's columns to the receiving vault,
straddle the Memorial's canons.

I close my hands around the sapling
honoring Stephen Walker –

Born in Greenwich,
Died in a distant land, says his plaque.

What if I die in a distant land
as our parents did?
Might I have a plaque one day?

We brush past cinnamon ferns, decipher
carvings on lichen-laced slate.

+
  Dawn Prior
 B 1901 ~ D 1922
Lost to Us in Australia
Brought Home to Rest

Oh Dawn, why Australia,
why that faraway place?

+
Who was this Flora, &
why a carved feather?
How sad her parents
had inscribed:

There fades a mother's fond delight
A father's brightest joy
And thus their mutual prospect bright
Does cruel death destroy.

+

Nehemia Doubleday
b. June 24, 1824
d. June 16, 1882

Bun's great-grandfather? Gracious!
May I never have to visit Bun here…

Will calls, *Listen to this:*

+

Elizabeth Ann Cutler
who suddenly departed this life
in an apoplectic fit
Sept. ye 2nd 1774

Is 'apoplectic,' like epilepsy?

I'm uncertain but inclined to satisfy:
-Remember when we found
Mrs. Zappey's cat staggering
in the roses, his mouth foamy?
An apoplectic fit's like that…
only worse.

We meander the rank grass; Will touches the marker
of a pauper's plot, sits near a yew.

I slide my palms across an unmarked stone,
wonder who was laid to rest un-mourned.

Maybe she was a Helen who sold potatoes & honey
or a Theo who mined soapstone on our mountain.

Perhaps she was like me, a Cora
who from the willow on her village green
watched sheep graze,
a girl who loved flowers.

I hold out my hand, pull up Will
from the pauper's side.

We cross the ravine to what remains of Enfield.

Shawl

All fall, Will wavers:
My legs want a horse,
my fingers want a kitten,
but my arms want a dog.

He names the collie Shawl
for the white of her shoulders
atop her russet fur.

We build her a house
beneath our elm, near the swing.
Blossom perches on its peak,
a feathered wind-vane.

I'd start a garden
to echo Shawl's coat –
trillium, calendula, anemone –
but I'd have to dig it up when we leave.

Saturdays, we race the dog
to Smith's Village – she wins.
I read *The Springfield Union*,
Shawl dozes beside the harness shop,
Will swaps "knock-knock" jokes
with Bun on the porch
of Swift River Hotel.

We stroll the field home.

Suddenly, the Body

Clifton Moore, the undertaker,
returned from Amherst to dig up

the grave markers & (on account
of frost-heaves) re-set them deep

at the QPC,
George Wesson's old farm –

corn stalks
now rows of monuments.

The dead hate disturbances, warns Will.
-Shush!

Back at Wood Lawn,
Mr. Moore & his crew

smooth their hoes over scant remains –
buttons, coffin handles, bits of bone.

I bend above an untouched grave.
Suddenly, the body:

a strand of dark dust
stretched along a pale band.

Gutted

A hunter left your head & hide
                              sliced off   flesh & hooves

where antlers sprung

        gored hollows //

Geese-call, leaf-scuttle

a beetle weaves through tufts toward your eye
                                    waggles away //

Last spring you dipped in

    & out of hostas

        in one leap cleared

            the hedge
            the lane //

Your tawny skin a folded cape

above Swift River –

                        Our towns stripped clean
                                gutted //

        Myrtle warbler's *tyew-tyew-tyew*

                glorious
                indifferent//

Amber

Our last Christmas on the farm,
we do what we've done
since they've been gone

Gramps centers the tree in the window,
Will strings garlands on the porch,
I fetch Mama's quilt which I drape

beneath the branches where it remains
while the soaked fruitcake's unwrapped,
holiday events scroll by

January 6th, it's washed &
carried to their bed
in that barren room…

My first quilt just begun,
I hold Mama's in my lap,
rest a palm on my square,

across my name, birth day,
a snowdrop above a drift

In a corner block: *Calvin & Cora*,
two hearts on a bell,
June 1, 1923

I fold my square to theirs –
for this moment,
then & now one

Mama wore a ring,
a bee preserved in resin.
I'm sealed in amber.

vowed not to cut my hair

'til the quilt's done but seems
my hair grows faster than I can stitch
now I flip it forward to braid it
March 15 + of 16 blocks 6 still aren't begun
sketched on the back of paper scraps
    *the elm & swing
    *Blossom on Shawl's rump
    *a gliding red-tailed hawk
    *our Flexible Flyers
    *Violet munching hay
    *a spider's web

Gramps brought down their trunk =
    Pa's denim work shirts, "Cal's Auto" on each
    Mama's dresses, mostly prints in blues

in a pocket found a folded recipe
showed Gramps who nodded, looked away…

snipped a 10-inch apron piece — one of its
lilies-of-the-valley faintly stained

was this what she baked their last day home?
embroidered the title on the square :

Lemon Pound Cake

Dana's Last Concert

Bernadine O'Gorman
from Worcester
stays with us after.

Shawl rests his head on her knee
while she tells us:

Such a sweet church, a small organ,
maybe 55 in attendance –
all had lost their homes.

There was a male singer plus
Danny Sylvester on the viola,
I on violin, of course.

When I'm 24,
like cousin Bernie,
I'll be a teacher, too –
I'll wear a cyclamen dress
& a tailored jacket.

We played ballads
as they don't need
particular accompaniment;

they were so appreciative –
oh, I wish
you could have heard it!

Her pageboy's side combs
catch the porch lamp's flicker.

It was the saddest program
I've ever been part of,
the saddest thing I've ever done.

Farewell Ball

They arrive, most in black,
crowds so vast the hall can't hold them:

the Grand March,
McEnnelly's Orchestra,

dancers spiraling across the lawn,
 Auld Lang Syne   then taps.

The clock's 12 strikes.
Sobs. Silence.

2 a.m. – Will asleep in the balcony
on a bench against the wall.

Gramps hoists him to his shoulder
like a slain lamb.

I swallow the cream-smooth night,
follow them home.

at 12:01 a.m.

*April 28, people were now in a town hall that
was no longer in a town that was no longer,
the Springfield Morning Union quoted a guest
from last night's Ball*

*if that isn't dizzying enough, Gramps says the lake will hold
412 billion gallons of water!*

$$412,000,000,000$$

EEK

*started a doodle – aimed to draw a teardrop for every gallon
gave up after five pages
1,848 per page, 9,240 tears in all**

*stopped because my hand numbed
& a powerful thirst overtook me
pumped a ladle of water from the well*

Opening Day

May 10 = we fished Chaffee Creek

later that week Miss Rugg introduced haiku **

as spring tumbled along I realized they're kin

> *fishing won't always mean catching*
> *trying haiku doesn't mean you write one*

for both I hold then release —
> *cast a lure beyond the fish,*
> *let the flow take it*
> *set down words composed in my head,*
> *more arrive, uninvited*

each harbors a secret —
> *one a wish,*
> *the other a dream*
> *the chatter of water over rock*
> *the silence when an image closes*

Irises

A stranger stops, asks for irises –
she points, meek at first,

as most wanting a favor begin,
bolder when something

assures the taking away releases –
I snip stalk after stalk,

air waffles between the flowers,
& I'm lightened.

The woman resembles an iris:
slender, erect, her scent

echoing that moment a blossom
begins to decay;

her presence
in the garden

becomes its central bloom,
anoints this day.

She walks off, bouquet
a wing in her arms;

I close the clippers,
clasp them:

Mama, I remember the autumn
you divided these bulbs,

settled the shorn halves,
watered them in.

Mrs. Munroe lowered the flag

on June 13 + Principal Ciccone
rang the bell 39 times —
for the years our school existed

each of us 9 graduates explained our projects —
I stood where mine hung, backing pinned,
on the wall behind the table with Will's model

This is my quilt — well, most of it, I said,
tried to sew places we could treasure:
Swift River, branches spread like reaching fingers

to 'Kreisler's Refrain,' we remembered Enfield,
lyrics by Miss Rugg

Mr. Gardner from Springfield
served up our area's history
peppered with names & dates

we received prizes (mine for writing)
Miss Rugg gave me a wrapped book*
then Dr. Segur, who's birthed every local baby some 40 + years,
presented our diplomas

guests mingled in the hall, admired our projects
nibbled a snickerdoodle ~
cider so cold my teeth clacked

road home glittered —
the full moon scaled Great Quabbin
slid her saffron face toward its summit

I'm immersed

in the book Miss Rugg gave me
~~~~~ ~~~~~~~~~~ ~~~~~~~~~~
saturated in words

stitched a white dress with
mother-of-pearl buttons

fixed a rope to our egg basket
lower it to the yard
when Will hollers for gingerbread

her free verse is a pot of tea steeped in metaphor

& – Gramps bought the Amherst house***

from **BOBBIN HOLLOW**

to RATTLESNAKE DEN

Cora Snow
Summer 1938

Dedicated to Bun Doubleday

　　　He weaves the hook
　　through the baby mouse's
　　　　pink neck

　　　　　　　　　　　　　　　The bullhead,
　　　　　　　　　　　　lip snared by a barb,
　　　　　　　　　　　　　　flexes its own

　　　　Suckers doze
　　too lazy to take the bait –
　　　our horse turns home

   Pan-fried, this flesh
feasted in the shallows last night
    below a butter moon

                                       Pickerel strung
                              across an alder branch
                                 burnished by rain

    Dawn
we hold our palms to the brook's brim –
     trout kiss them

E.D. ~ C.S.

She pressed flowers as do I.

She's named for her mother, so am I.

She had long, chestnut hair just like mine.

When we're settled on Main Street
across from the Homestead,
I'll watch her windows for a spell,
write…

I'll be buried in West Cemetery, too –

a simple stone, just *C.S.*

She wrote,
> *Art- a House that tries to be haunted –*

I'm writing toward whatever that means.

no parade

this July 4 unless you count trailers headed
away always away from town piled with lumber,
furniture, even Cyprian Uracious's house!

other years Will & Bun would be whooping it up
chucking poppers on bricks
stuffing crackers under stumps to blow them up –
no Roman candles fizzling on the mountain tonight

Gramps appeared from the cellar with – sparklers**
I plonked a watermelon in the milk room cooling-tank
went swimming with Bun

things could be worse

III. Spring 1943 ~ Summer 1946

+ Adelaide

I roam where
Will & I played

when through fog
a girl emerges

from the unmarked stone
by the pauper's plot.

She tosses her ponytail, taps
a riding crop against boots.

*I'm Adelaide. We were
both 14 when we died.*

-Only just… Back then,
I wondered if you grew potatoes.

*I know what you wondered.
A snake spooked my horse*

*which reared then trotted on home.
My parents never found me.*

*Years later, workers clearing Pelham Hollow
 unearthed my bones.*

-I'd like to find my parents,
at least know where, or if, they are.

I had that hunger once.

+ Popcorn Snow

I linger near Asa's plot
until he ascends,
through slant snow
follow him to Petersham where
we let ourselves down.

Asa's farm re-forms –
a goat prances to him,
tail a-wag, as if it were
hours since she'd seen him,
not seventy years.

A tipped stool materializes,
two lengths of knotted serge:

As I left for town that morning,
Isabelle was milking;
I leaned on the Dutch door,
told her I wouldn't be long.

"Don't forget my thread," she said,
started to add something,
didn't.

I returned
to a stillness.
These dress hem strips?
Must have tried twice…
tenacious…

Thought ours'd been a decent life,
though nothing's perfect…
Had an elaborate tomb built,
put the thread in her coffin.

The serge diminishes,
rafters then loft.
In the kitchen – a chair,
table with pitcher & bowl.

*I'd been Asa all my life;
when I took to having
popcorn in milk for supper,
the neighbors' nickname held.*

He points to the stoop.
*I was carrying a dressed pig,
died right here.
In that instant I wondered,
will I see Isabelle when I cross over?*

Sorrow seeps from him
like mist.

*I'd arranged for the undertaker
to check for a week,
be certain I was gone.*

*For a long while,
my body lay in Dana
in a zinc coffin
with a half-top window.*

*One day Cob Powers
smashed the glass,
stole my diamond tie-pin
right off this lapel.*

*Old Cob got a fright,
& he deserved it:
when that night air hit,
 my face puckered,
 just like that.*

We coast the stippled fields
  to our snow-mounded graves.

Maybe the coffin kept her from me,
or because she chose death
it was a surer exit.

All I know is I'm still here,
& Isabelle isn't.

Sleight

Back there, I once
drew thousands of tears

This bobcat dozing
on a ledge
knows nothing of grief

I let myself into her
where her steady heart
soothes me

How our fur
shimmers in this light

+ Flora Howe

B May 5, 1903 ~
D November 25, 1918

Across from hers, my stone's
chiseled snowdrop &

just the word *Cora,*
as if more might erase me

In a world absorbed by this one,
I'd admired the carved feather –

now frost etches its tips
while she recalls

My last day, Father brought
the bird to our porch –

he bore it as he'd once held me,
my face beneath an eyelet bonnet,

its head lolled, nestled
in his elbow's curve,

eyes the same glazed grey
as our breathing.

He dropped it on the bench: that thud
as snow slips through branches.

I pulled off my mittens, tried
to warm my hands beneath it,

shivered while he bound
its legs with twine.

*He plucked a plume then hung
it from the ceiling hook:*

*I watched the pheasant twirl,
touched its feather to my chin.*

A Word That Breathes

of the distant war
whispered above daffodils
at E.D.'s grave

I wait a while
above her iron rail
but she's not there

in their side garden
Gramps & Will
sow seeds

under frail sun
their arms gilded
their motions spare

a wind like curry
brought me to Amherst
whisks me away

✝ Annie E. Doane

B 1872 ~ D 1897

She was beautiful
in the way a storm can be,
& a blizzard raged
while she spoke:

He'd lived past what I lived for

yet in the obsidian
of the year's last night,
the desire seized me
to take him a tissue-wrapped pear;

the horse startled
as I plucked its moon-soaked rein,

my song's notes
skittered toward sheep
whose muzzles
snow disfigured.

Sleet coiled
on silos –
how he'd wound my hair
around his hand –

& what lies forgotten
between rime-rimmed furrows?

Cold muted
the mountain for good,
crags silenced
like stitched mouths.

I went to him already ruined.

Isn't It Time

I zipped to a lower limb,
Asa followed:

Isn't it time you spoke it?

The cedar groaned in the wind.

-Why say what seems a lie –
this place, you, my truth now?

*Perhaps to make what's become unreal
alive again.*

I swirled. The wind sighed.

*Be still, Cora.
Be calm.*

-A gap deformed the hills,
Enfield a fire-pocked crater,
our family one of five still there.

The ancient beech felled,
hacked into chunks. Smoke insinuated

the woolen mill, poked at the town hall's
vacant eyes, huffed above us,
the way in the past clouds moved.

I'd spread my finished quilt
on the parched grass. We took
turns feeding the fire,
Shawl wagging her tail but whimpering.

The valley heaved with fever,
embers squinted, hissed …

I leaned,
then wind,
a gust,

with a root
in my hand
I leaned,

the root
like a claw, just

as I turned
to fling it,

flames
took my skirt

A Sudden Freight of Wind

presages Bun's arrival

he falls to the snow

his sob-sighs
like wing throbs
when swans rise

each visit
he fixes on my name

with the then eyes
of our young selves

that lived reality
spectral now

my desire beyond reach

to convey there's
nothing to express

bound
to the urge to express it

Pale Scar

They've been building
a brick tower

to overlook
this wilderness,

& now it's done.

I sky-scale it,
conjure our towns –
mere hill tips
whose leaves shudder.

The water
creeps upward
in this somber
reservoir
Frank Winsor
termed a solution

but we knew
foretold oblivion.

I angle lower,
closer to Enfield –

its sinuous road
a pale scar

whose curves
I trace
on air.

+ Dawn Prior

B 1901 ~ D 1922
Lost to Us in Australia
Brought Home to Rest

She only awoke when it rained,
never spoke. She'd hold her arms
away from her sides, the way
anhingas spread their plumage to dry.

In drizzle I tell her,
-I like rain,
prefer it to fire.
Fire was my undoing.

She glares,
shifts so her palms
face the sky,
leans back her head,
lets her mouth go slack.

-I never left Massachusetts,
still haven't. Australia.
A faraway place.

She lowers her hands, turns:

Alice Springs was arid,
almost a desert,
its river ephemeral.
In the end, there was rain –

rain on MacDonnell Range,
in its gorge, rain
on its quartzite peaks,
all night someone sketched
rivulets with a silver pen,

*six hours of dingo howl,
of galahs' chit-chit
as they bounced
between jacarandas,
their heads, rosebuds;*

*I listened for the fugitive river,
the Todd's upstream gush
over ochre, for the moment
froth churned into town,*

*suddenly it was rustling along
like an opaque gown
while Arrernte dunted
spikes through mud –
toothpicks into mocha cake,
it flashed
toward Heavitree Gap,
gathered favors
in its rumpled skirt:
chrysoprase chunks,
mulga woomera,
a bloodwood trunk
whose coccids traversed
its invisible avenues;*

*I willed the vanishing
stay visible,
but my body relented,
submerged,*

*the flood's crest
pulled me beneath
Taffy Pick bridge
& the last thing
I would see:*

*a honeyeater
chittering on the rail.*

What Was Said

Asa said, *I imagined I'd see God's face, if God has one*
        I said -I thought light would consume me, not fire

Time passes, but we appear exempt
        -Perhaps we cleave until we understand

Some suggest we're on earth to learn
        -She read Emerson

Our souls endure
        -She wrote the soul selects then shuts the door

The myths-- allegorical, spiritual
        -Where have some of these souls gone

At times this feels infinite; at others, interminable
        -Could they have been absorbed

To die might be to sleep, then wake in a newborn's body
        -I used to dream I was a stag

Are we trapped because our deaths were unexpected
        -What if I closed the valves of my attention

We're stuck or holding on
        -like stone

We exist in those who remember us
        -I exist to remember what I loved

This might be all
        -I might go home

IV. 1947 ~ ~ ~

At Last

Restless above
the brittle shore

I study the lake's
uncomplicated brow,

her chiaroscuro so irresistible,
I dive –

the water's weight
insistent, intimate –

I want to drown
in her embrace,

I plunge,
arrive at last

in what's become
of Enfield.

At First

I keep to the gate
   which rusts at a pace
      that makes
         this space predictable

Iron filigrees drop
  in slow motion
     as in autumns when
        leaves twirled toward
           playgrounds & streams

I push off
  from the pillars
    which framed it
       before they released Swift River
        & this became a spliced hulk
           canoeists glimpse on dank days

Back then Will & I
  swung on the open halves
     our fingers gripped curlicues
     our toes skimmed dirt

I venture out then back
  from this landmark
    the way Mill Pond's shed
      was my measure
        of how far I'd swum
          how many gulps of air
            would carry me home

Now I rely on the gate
  as a compass point
    for above in all directions
      this inscrutable lake.

Hollyhocks

They were what I loved best
about Enfield summers –

                their heart-shaped, tufted leaves,
                maroon blooms
                which noon thinned pink

                I'd step between budded stalks &

                              beneath arched spindles
                              become another outline
                              stenciled on our barn door

Now, fifteen fathoms
press against this garden,

                water that bleached
                the pastels from the valley,
                stifled the bumblebees' hum,
                the sparrow's hymn

                Within this silence

                              I invoke the hollyhocks'
                              wind-rustle,
                              their seed-pods' rattle
                              as I shook them free

What fire didn't slay,
time has,

                but even it
                can never erode
                what I remember

All Afternoon

I backstroke
below the slope
where lilacs blur

A squall's sizzle
evokes the *tap-thwat-tat*
of bubbling jam…

                That last July, we waded
                through blueberries,
                swung our pails, unaware –

                with what casual joy
                we carried that final harvest
                home…

Here's that family on the shore again,
lifting from their hamper
a bowl of fruit;
the parents read, the children
play catch with a peach –

the boy's toss overshoots his sister,
the peach sinks,
passes me,
settles on rubble.

All afternoon
I trail rainbow trout,
sun strumming their fins,
halt where berries grew,
surge on.

Water-boatman

I favor the light diffused through firs,
    its slow tinting of the roads' remains

as day fades. At first I believed
    myself transformed,

yet that truth unraveled. Now, paused
    above the old meadow,

its fescue long-swallowed, I consider
    the span between here & heaven –

if such a place exists of itself, or
    if it's a state of my contrivance.

Ripples re-shape the red-winged blackbirds,
    the muffled trill of *conk-a-ree*

I chase swallow shadows
    on the ceiling of our drowned town,

recall their flicker on hyacinths,
    forsythia, the sweet-peas of June,

the times I buried my face
    in hydrangeas. I follow the

water-boatman whose hind legs, like tiny
    oars, propel him from air & sun

to water & shade – how casual
    his navigation between spaces,

as if one could exist in both present & past.
    As if it were that simple.

((((Halo))))

With the storm passed
the stag comes back
to drink at the bank

I keep close
while his tongue like ink
dips in & out

From the moon
grace
a ring of light

Finding Swift River

The lake glints, a blade my strokes sharpen,
each exhale a coin spun across its dark
as my arms churn black to gold

I follow each chill articulation through
streams, ponds, the river's branches,
my body a shadow above Greenwich then Dana,

it's October again, our mountains now islands
I circle, maples igniting the peaks of
Mt. Pomeroy & Curtis Hill

I move beneath ice come December,
the chop above Prescott frozen meringue where
an eagle fastens on a doe's carcass, tarsi lifting flesh,

then all through May, what had been emerges:
bonnet factories, billiard-leg makers, Conkey's Tavern
beyond which a door opens –

A Door Opens

on our house –
white as a dress left on the line –
& time transmutes

the church bells' nine slow tolls: a man has died

a note brought to school
read to our class
The ice is safe on Mill Pond

the bells toll five times: a woman has died

Scott Prentice
stands in the sugar house
boiling his final sap run

two bell tolls: a child has died

the rabbit train hops to a stop
to let out Dr. Mary Walker
in top hat, tails, & cane

the bells' nine tolls, their five, their two

in the oldest section of his orchard
George Webster savors the last apples –
one Search No Further, two Crows Eggs

the church bells' nine slow tolls: a man has died;
five tolls, a woman; two, a child

I never heard the bells
that tolled for me.

Vespers

                            I float

dragonflies   stir   this   brew

        tanagers flit onto ash   burn into pine

drop

    to pickerel   sugaring silt   a turtle edging   away

              flutter-kick

      through   chimney smoke

pass   hog pen   barn   porch

glide   into the kitchen

                                lift   the cup

      drink

    yellow beauty-mark   of water-lily

                raspberry's   dusky tang

    repeat   with chocolate-voiced frogs

        our litany   of loss

we drift   through   leafcloudflame

sing   with all our hearts   for what remains

Currents

Ice-melt trickle
on Pottapaug's edge

surface figures
gleam

The sachem waits
with his stag

their eyes
find mine

NaniQuaben kneels
gives thanks

he slips his hands
past the pond's face

I rise
take them

Acknowledgments

Thank you to the following publications in which these poems appeared, sometimes in earlier versions or with different titles:

Cape Cod Poetry Review
"A Door Opens," "Finding Swift River"

Journal of the Washington Center for Psychoanalysis
"Popcorn Snow," "Water-boatman," "Wisps," "Vespers"

PoetryLife
"Annie E. Doane"

Prime Time
"Flora Howe"

roger
"At Last"

The MacGuffin
"Gutted"

World of Water, World of Sand
"Irises"

Source Notes

Phrases occasionally were incorporated into Cora's poems and journal entries. These were drawn from tapes, books, interviews, writers' works, and museums. *Water~Dreaming*'s narrative was enriched by these, and I'm indebted to them.

~Samuel Beckett, Emily Dickinson, Joan Houlihan, & James Joyce.
~Interview with Bernadine O'Gorman Sullivan, 94, at her Harwich, Massachusetts home, November 2, 2009.
~Phone interview with Daniel Otis Parker, Colorado, in June of 2015. Daniel lived in Greenwich from 1931-38. The legendary grandfather's clock, inspiration for the classic song of the same name, has been in his family since 1790.
~Taped interviews on "Here Was Home," with former Swift River Valley residents. Written and narrated by Lisa Yeisley.
~From a large collection of taped interviews of former Swiss River Valley residents compiled by Audrey Rosalind Duckert: recollections of George Boynton of Enfield, recorded by her on May 20, 1974.
~Quabbin Visitor & Information Center, Winsor Dam, the Reservoir.
~Special Collections Library at University of Massachusetts Amherst.
~The Homestead, Amherst, Massachusetts.
~The New England Quilt Museum, Lowell, Massachusetts.
~The Swift River Historical Society, North New Salem, Massachusetts.

Works:

The Creation of Quabbin Reservoir: The Death of the Swift River Valley; J.R. Greene. The Transcript Press. 1981.
The Dickinsons of Amherst; Jerome Liebling and Christopher Benfey. University Press of New England. 2001.
Letters from Quabbin: The Springfield Union: April 14, 1938-July 19, 1938; Friends of Quabbin, Incorporated. 1991.
Quabbin: The Accidental Wilderness; Thomas Conuel. Massachusetts Audubon Society. 1981.

With Gratitude

~ to Jane Yolen's *Letting Swift River Go*, illustrated by Barbara Cooney; this haunting picture book, which I opened for the first time in 1992, inspired me to find my way of telling this story.

~ for the deep attention to craft by the generous, wise Bass River Revisionists who've been honing my poems' blades for twenty years. They include: Susan Berlin, John Bonanni, Jack Harrison, Kate Mele, Mary Ellen Redmond, and Lauren Wolk.

~oh, EZs!

~ to summer workshop leaders at the Fine Arts Work Center and to winter ones at The Palm Beach Poetry Festival. Special thanks to Tony Hoagland. Finest teacher. Ever.

~ to my New Directions colleagues.

~ for Angela Howes, Bass River Press's editor, whose 20-15 vision fine-tuned each detail.

~ to Martha Rhodes, who on August 20, 2017, at Colrain's Manuscript Conference asked me one question which changed everything.

~ and to Father William Ryan who wrote in the margin of a poem draft in 1978, "Give me something to start my new life."

About the Author

Deirdre Grace Callanan's poems and essays have appeared in such periodicals as *Beloit Poetry Journal, Colorado Review,* and *Poet Lore*. She began her teaching career in Virginia's Northern Neck in 1970 and subsequently taught in Colorado, Northern Virginia, Washington, DC, and on Cape Cod. During her year as the Massachusetts Christa McAuliffe Fellow, she wrote a text for educators, *Windows & Mirrors: Writing's Power for Illumination & Reflection*. Since 2006, she has served on the writing faculty at the Washington Center for Psychoanalysis.

www.ingramcontent.com/pod-product-compliance
Lightning Source LLC
Chambersburg PA
CBHW051956290426
44110CB00015B/2265